STICKER BOOK

Maurice Pledger

WILDLIFE WORLD

Over 200 colorful stickers

Silver Dolphin
San Diego, California

Silver Dolphin Books
An imprint of the Baker & Taylor Publishing Group
10350 Barnes Canyon Road, San Diego, CA 92121
www.silverdolphinbooks.com

This edition published in 2010
First edition published in 2002

ISBN-13: 978-1-60710-170-3
ISBN-10: 1-60710-170-X

Made in Malaysia

2 3 4 5 14 13 12 11 10

About this book

Get ready to be a sticker collector! On the following pages you can learn about all kinds of creatures—interesting insects, beautiful birds, and amazing mammals are all waiting to be discovered.

Turn to the back of the book, and you'll find lots of stickers, too. Use them to complete the sticker activities on every page by filling in the animal shapes or making up your own pictures of the wonderful world of animals.

★ All kinds of CREATURES

The world is full of all kinds of creatures. Some have fur or feathers. Some have wings or beaks or shells. Here you can see Oscar Otter and his friend Dilly Dormouse. They are both **mammals**. On Oscar's back you can see Olivia Owl and Sally Cygnet. They are both **birds**.

What other creatures can you see in the picture?

Can you see a butterfly? Or a beetle? Butterflies and beetles both belong to a group of animals called **insects**. On the following pages you can find out about the most common groups of animals that live in our world. You'll meet all sorts of wonderful creatures—and don't forget to use your stickers as you go!

★ All sorts of INSECTS

Down in the meadow, Billy Bunny and his friend Charlie Chick have found all sorts of insects. You can find out their names on the next few pages. Use your stickers to add a flying beetle and a honeybee to the picture.

Beetles, bees, and other insects

Charlie Chick loves to go looking for insects. You can see lots of different ones here. Look for them in your garden, especially in the summer.

Beetles

Use your stickers to fill in the shapes with the right insects. You can fill them all in now or wait until you see each different type of creature.

Bumblebees

Honeybee

Hoverfly

Wasp

Bee flies

Flies

Grasshoppers

⭐ Other creepy-crawlies

Apart from insects, there are lots of other creepy-crawly creatures. Do you already know the names of some of the ones shown here?

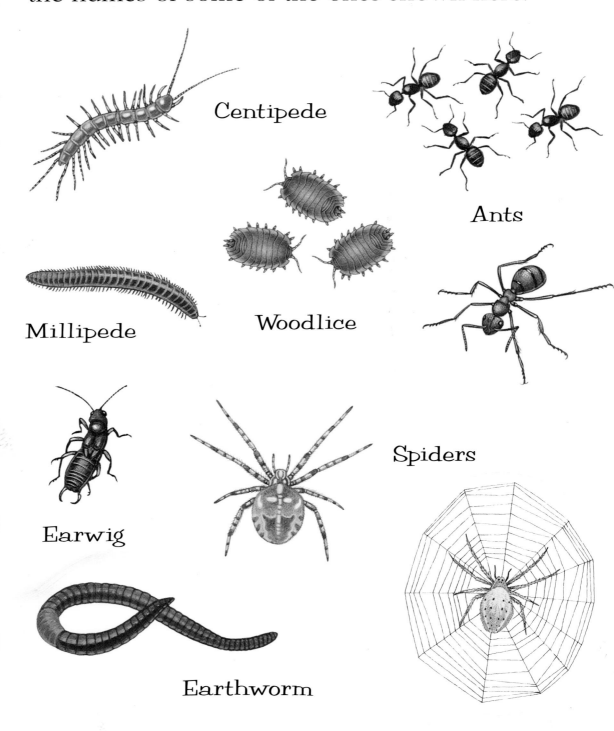

Centipede

Ants

Woodlice

Millipede

Spiders

Earwig

Earthworm

Say the creepy-crawlies' names as you fill in the shapes with the right stickers.

Snails

Slugs

DID YOU KNOW
that caterpillars are
actually baby butterflies?
They change into chrysalides
before turning into adults.
This process is called
"metamorphosis."

Chrysalides

Caterpillars

Butterflies and moths

Butterflies and moths are some of the most colorful insects of all. Their wings are often covered in fantastic patterns.

Butterflies

Use your stickers to fill in these shapes with different butterflies and moths.

Moths

DID YOU KNOW that most moths fly at night? But the cinnabar moth (below) flies during the day!

Pond insects

★

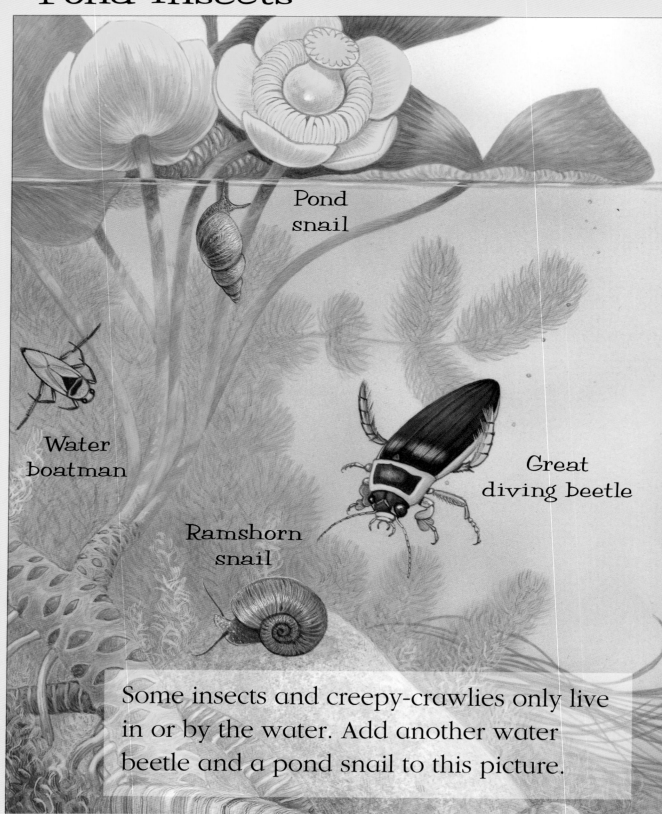

Pond
snail

Water
boatman

Ramshorn
snail

Great
diving beetle

Some insects and creepy-crawlies only live
in or by the water. Add another water
beetle and a pond snail to this picture.

★

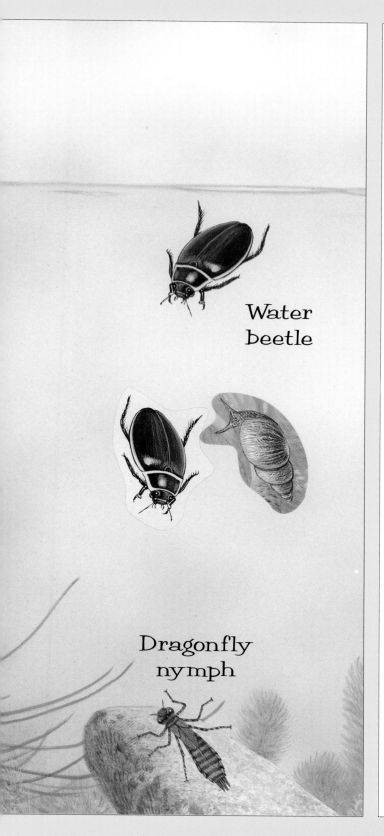

Water
beetle

Dragonfly
nymph

Look for these
flying insects by
ponds and rivers.

Damselfly

Mayfly

Darter
dragonfly

Hawker dragonfly

REPTILES and AMPHIBIANS

Oscar Otter and Dora Duckling are looking
for two other sorts of creatures by the river–reptiles
and amphibians. Find out about them over the next
few pages, then add another frog and a terrapin to
the picture.

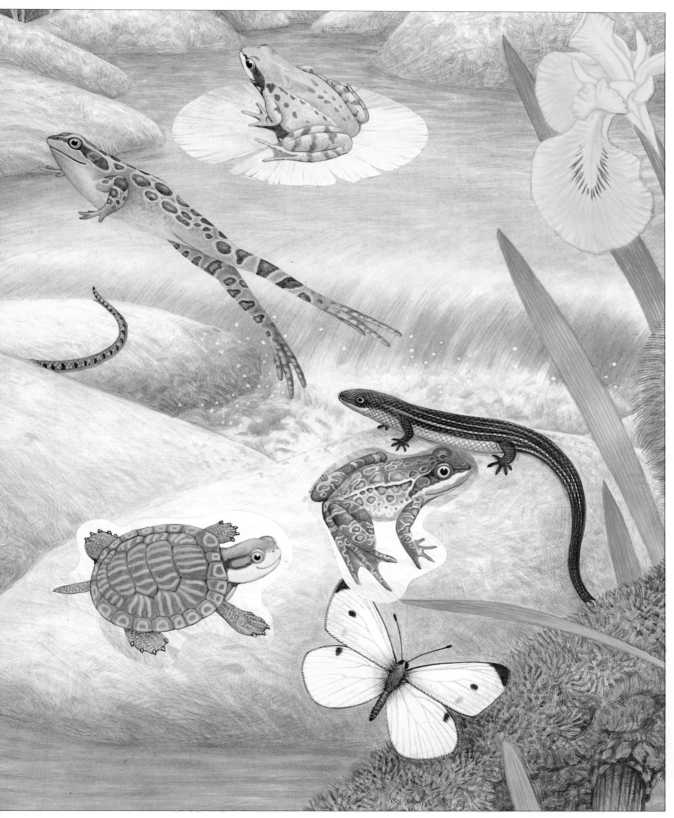

Snakes, frogs, and other friends

Look at the different reptiles and amphibians that Oscar Otter and Dora have found. Use your stickers to fill in their shapes.

Lizard

Tortoise

These creatures are all reptiles.

Turtle

Terrapin

Snake

Reptiles and amphibians both lay eggs. Frogs' eggs are called "spawn."

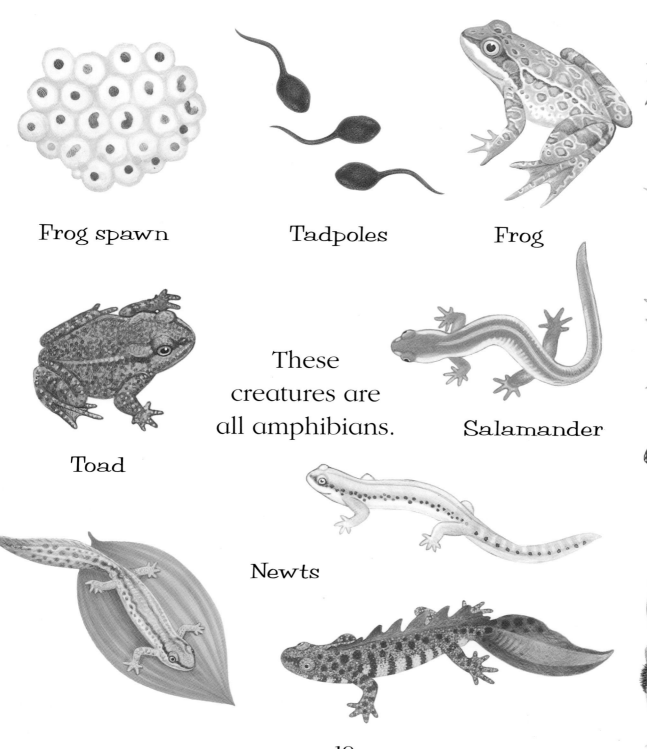

Frog spawn

Tadpoles

Frog

Toad

These creatures are all amphibians.

Salamander

Newts

All kinds of FISH

Many different kinds of fish live in ponds and rivers. Dotty Dragonfly likes to look for them when she's flying above the water. Add two more fish from your sticker sheet to the picture.

Freshwater fish

Dotty Dragonfly's favorite fish is the goldfish. Did you know that all wild goldfish have come from pet goldfish that people have set free in ponds and rivers?

Goldfish

Goby

Pike

Carp

Use your stickers to fill in these shapes with different freshwater fish.

Salmon

Bluegill

Zander

Stickleback

Dace

All sorts of BIRDS

Little Jenny Wren is looking for some of her bird friends in the field. Use your stickers to add two more birds to the picture.

Feathered friends

★ Jenny Wren has many different types of bird friends. They are all covered in feathers. Make a list of the birds that visit your garden. Can you see any of them pictured here?

Hummingbird

Blue tit

Sparrow

Quail

Goldfinch

Use your stickers to fill in the shapes of Jenny Wren's feathered friends.

Jackdaw

Goldcrest

Swallow

Woodpecker

Oystercatcher

Crossbill

Seagull

Pigeon

Masters of the skies

Some of these big birds are quite rare. You might see them flying over mountains and other high ground. Now add another bald eagle and a falcon from your sticker sheet to the picture.

Golden eagle

Bald eagle

Hawk

Kestrel

Here are some more birds to look for.

Barn owl

Falcon

Buzzard

Tawny owl chick

⭐ Birds who live by the water

Many birds live by rivers, ponds, and lakes. Some spend most of the time swimming in the water, even when it is freezing cold!

Goose

Kingfisher

Egret

Heron

Use your stickers to fill in the shapes with some different waterbirds.

Duckling

Duck

Swan

Cygnet

DID YOU KNOW that "cygnet" is the name for a baby swan?

Wood duck

All sorts of MAMMALS

Like most mammals, Billy Bunny is covered in fur. See how many furry friends he has found down in the woods. Now add two more mammals from your sticker sheet to the picture.

Mice and small mammals

Here are some of Billy Bunny's small mammal friends. They are often hard to spot in the wild because they are good at hiding from people!

Field mouse

Wood mice

Bat

Dormouse

Use your stickers to fill in the animal shapes.

Stoats

Weasel

Hare

Mole

Squirrels

More furry friends

Bobby Bear has found some bigger mammals down by the old log. Now use your stickers to add a possum and a chipmunk to the scene.

Wolf

Raccoon

Bear

Here are three more creatures to watch out for!

Fox

Badger

Deer

Riverbank friends

Billy Bunny has found some more furry friends down by the river. See them in the panel opposite, then use your stickers to add an otter and a water vole to the picture.

Use your stickers
to fill in the shapes.

Otter

Water
vole

Beaver

All sorts of SEA LIFE

On the next few pages you will find all sorts of
special creatures that are only found by the sea.
Find a striped fish and a starfish on your sticker
sheet and add them to the picture.

On the beach

Sidney Seal loves looking for creatures along the seashore and in rock pools. Use your stickers to fill in the pictures of the things he has found.

Shrimp

Starfish

Sand dollar

Sea fan

Sea urchins

And don't forget to see how many of the things pictured here you can find the next time you go to the beach.

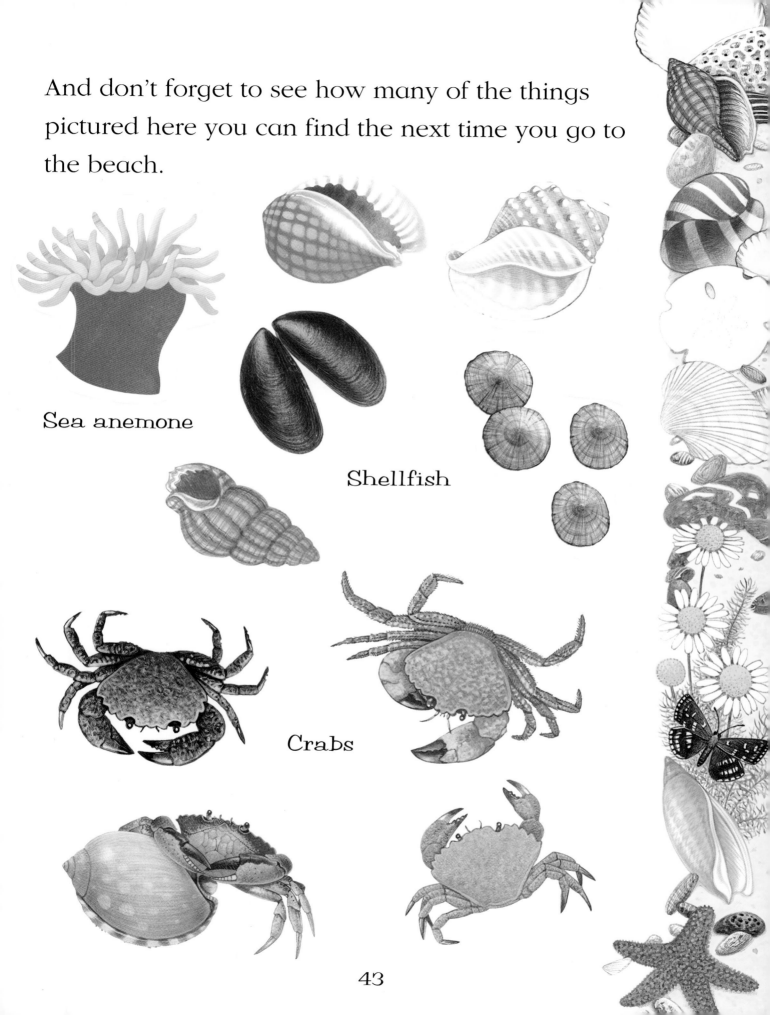

Sea anemone

Shellfish

Crabs

Under the sea!

Sidney Seal likes to dive into the ocean to find more interesting creatures. Use your stickers to fill in the shapes of the things he has seen beneath the waves.

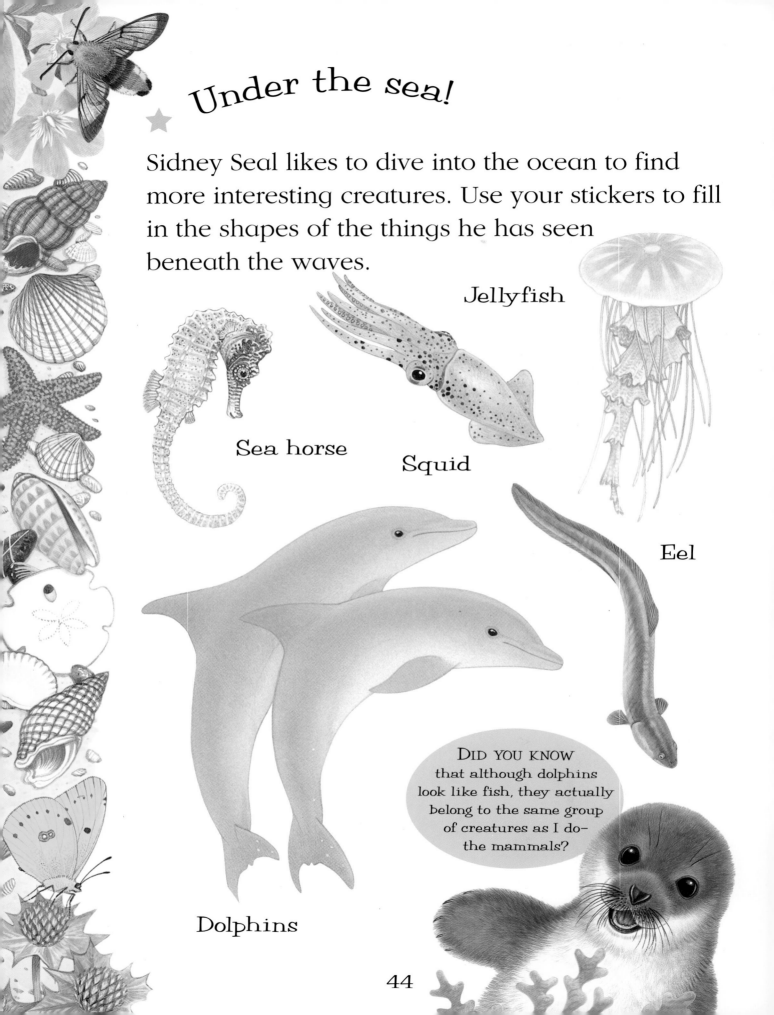

Jellyfish

Sea horse

Squid

Eel

Dolphins

DID YOU KNOW that although dolphins look like fish, they actually belong to the same group of creatures as I do— the mammals?

44

Look for these fish if you ever visit
an aquarium.

Fish

Shark

★ Make your own picture!

Can you remember the names of all of the creatures shown here? If you can't, look back in the book to find them. Now use your stickers to make up your own picture of all kinds of creatures.

How to use your stickers

Look for the page numbers on the sticker sheets to help you find the right stickers for the different activities in this book. Peel each one carefully from its backing sheet and use it to fill in the shapes or add to the pictures. You can also use your stickers to record the animals you see in real life. Look for the creatures in this book when you're outside, then fill in their sticker shapes as you see them. Some animals are easier to spot than others. Some may not live where you do, so look for them when you visit the zoo. Soon you'll find your whole book is complete. Then you'll be a champion sticker collector!

Add to scene on pages 6–7

Page 8

Page 9

Page 9

Page 10

Page 11